Jo Morris has represented servicemen in Germany, Colchester and in Aldershot. She has an intimate knowledge of the Armed Forces Act and other relevant legislation and her military background gives her an advantage over others when defending servicemen. She is also well acquainted with operational law and the law of armed conflict.

Libby Anderson has represented service personnel in the UK. She has particular interest in how the international law of armed conflict is adapting to the new challenges posed by cyber warfare, drones, social media and open source intelligence, and changes in the geopolitical landscape. She is familiar with the Armed Forces Act 2006 and other aspects of civilian law, such as the Data Protection Act 1998 and the Regulation of Investigatory Powers Act 2000, which affect military operations.

A Practical Guide to the Law of Military Justice

A Practical Guide to the Law of Military Justice

Jo Morris
BA, MA, PG Dip
Barrister, Charter Chambers

Libby Anderson
BA, MA, PG Dip, LLM
Barrister, Charter Chambers

Law Brief Publishing

Published 2020 by Law Brief Publishing, an imprint of Law Brief Publishing Ltd
30 The Parks
Minehead
Somerset
TA24 8BT

www.lawbriefpublishing.com

Paperback: 978-1-911035-62-6

PREFACE

This book was written with a range of audiences in mind. The authors wished to provide a book addressing the essential features of the law and practice of military justice in England and Wales, and hope that students, practitioners, and Assisting Officers alike may be assisted by this guide.

The first edition of this book states the law as at 2 September 2020.

Jo Morris
Libby Anderson
September 2020

CONTENTS

CHAPTER ONE
INTRODUCTION

This book is intended as a brief guide for the busy practitioner to military justice. It does not and cannot amount to a comprehensive work, but it can provide a broad outline to the issues faced by most of us who practice in the military arena.

The need for military justice is clear. Greater discipline is required to create an effective fighting force than the civilian law allows. Service personnel are held to a higher standard than civilians and for good reason. Further they are stationed all over the world in locations where the UK would not have jurisdiction. Without a distinct system of military justice, law and order in the forces would be impossible.

It is important at this early stage to draw a distinction between Disciplinary Action and Administrative Action. Disciplinary Action encompasses proceedings in the Service Criminal Justice System, including Service custody, summary hearing, Court Martial and Appeal, under statutory powers. Administrative Action is action taken by commanders using their authority under Queen's Regulations to safeguard or restore operational effectiveness. Administrative Action is governed by AGAI-67. This book is primarily concerned with the former, although there is a relationship between the two that will be explored in due course.

The following key abbreviations will be used throughout:

AFA	Armed Forces Act 2006
AFCLAA	Armed Forces Criminal Legal Aid Authority
CMAC	Court Martial Appeal Court

CO	Commanding Officer
DAO	Defence Assisting Officer
JA	Judge Advocate
JAG	Judge Advocate General
MOD	Ministry of Defence
NCO	Non-Commissioned Officer
PACE	Police and Criminal Evidence Act 1984
RAF	Royal Air Force
RN	Royal Navy
SCJS	Service Criminal Justice System
SPA	Service Prosecuting Authority
SP	Service person/service personnel

A brief history of the Court Martial

The modern-day Court Martial has its origin in the ancient principles of the medieval chivalric code. The original authority for the enforcement of military justice derived from the royal prerogative. In the medieval period, the court with jurisdiction over the conduct of soldiers was the Court of the High Constable and Earl Marshal. In the Early Modern period, it became known as the 'Court of the Marshal'.

The first Judge Advocate General, hereafter the JAG, was appointed in 1666. The JAG was responsible for supervising courts-martial following the creation of a standing army, known as the New Model Army, in 1645. The tradition of the JAG prevails but the nature of the role has changed enormously. Originally the JAG occupied a purely advisory role to lay members of the panel similar to that of the Magistrates' Court clerk. The office of the JAG still exists today, with responsibility for the Court-martial process.

Historically, the naval courts-martial system was entirely separate to the system developing under the JAG. The office of Judge Advocate of the Fleet (JAF) was established by the Naval Discipline Act 1661 to supervise discipline in the Royal Navy.

These early courts had jurisdiction only over English soldiers, but the role of the courts-martial spread in line with the territory, covering first England, then Great Britain in the wake of King James VI and I, then the United Kingdom after the Act of Union 1801, assuming responsibility for the Army and the Royal Navy, and in the 20th century the Royal Flying Corps which of course became the Royal Air Force we know today. The court-martial now has jurisdiction for all British land, air and naval forces overseas.

The Mutiny Act of 1689 formally recognised the authority of the JAG and the Service Courts, whose power was strengthened by the passing of successive Acts over the next two centuries. The next major development was the passing of the Army Act 1881, which replaced the principal provisions of the Mutiny Acts, and has been renewed every five years since that date to reflect changes in civil law. Three Service Discipline Acts were introduced in the 1950s, providing a comprehensive system of Service law incorporating civilian criminal offences, and offences that were unique to the Armed Forces.

The legislation currently in force is the Armed Forces Act 2006, which came into effect on 31 October 2009. The Act created a single system of Service law, repealing the three Service Discipline Acts of 1955/57, amalgamating the traditional offices of JAG and JAF into the single JAG we recognise today, and establishing the Court Martial as a standing court.

The modern Court Martial

The modern-day court martial was brought into being by the Armed Forces Act 2006. Originally they were ad hoc and could be convened anywhere, including the theatre of war, and dissolved subsequently. Section 154 of the Act created a standing court martial with jurisdiction to try any Service offence across all British land, air and naval forces including civilians subject to service discipline. 'Service offence' incorporates all criminal conduct offences and disciplinary, or non-criminal offences, as defined in section 50(2) of the Armed Forces Act 2006. However, civilians subject to Service discipline may be tried only for a restricted list of disciplinary offences.

The court martial, in dealing with service offences, largely mirrors civilian the criminal justice system. The arrest and investigation is covered by PACE 1984 and subsequent amendments with only minor variations. The commanding officer or subordinate officer can hear minor military offences and certain civilian offences in the same way that the magistrates can hear summary only matters. More serious offences are the remit of the Court Martial and the appeal avenues are broadly the same as the civilian system.

Summary dealing remains the remit of a Commanding Officer, hereafter CO, or a subordinate officer. COs are able to deal with service personnel for minor criminal offences and certain civilian offences. Those charges capable of being heard by the CO are set out in S52-54 of the Armed Forces Act 2006. Either way offences can be found at Schedule 1, Part 1 of the Armed Forces Act 2006 and those offences that allow the CO to proceed only with permission at Schedule 1, Part of AFA 2006.

Summary hearings are designed for petty offences but not trivial matters, and are relatively informal affairs. The accused person has various rights. He can admit or deny the offence and has the assistance of an officer. He also has the right to appeal sentence and conviction to the Court Martial. COs have no legal training and no assistance upon the law but have limited powers. COs can also delegate to subordinate officers. In those circumstances they have they can take "minor administrative action" which mirrors the punishments open to any employer for misbehaving employees.

COs, however, can reduce service personnel by one rank, fine or imprison for up to twenty-eight days without permission from any person. With permission he can detain for up to ninety days.

Practicalities

Much of what happens in the courts-martial will seem familiar to criminal practitioners, either because the procedure is the same or is directly analogous to what happens in the civilian courts. One of the most helpful things a civilian practitioner can do will be to become familiar with military language and terminology.

The Service Prosecuting Authority, headed by the Director of Service Prosecutions, is the equivalent of the Crown Prosecution Service. The SPA was formed on 1 January 2009 with the incorporation of the Navy Prosecution Authority, Army Prosecuting Authority and Royal Air Force Prosecuting Authority. It reviews cases referred to it by the Service Police or Chain of Command, then initiates and conducts appropriate criminal prosecutions involving alleged offences contrary to military discipline. It works in the service courts of first instance and acts as respondent in the service appellate courts. The SPA sits within the Ministry of Defence under the remit of the Attorney General, and is fully independent of the military chain of command.

Prosecution counsel tends to be drawn from the pool of legal counsel within the relevant branch of the Services, essentially in-house counsel. For the Army, for example, this would be the Army Legal Services. Counsel from within the Services will hold commissioned officer rank, having either completed a pupillage or training contract in the civilian justice system before undertaking Professionally Qualified Officer training, or else will have been sponsored through their legal training and military training by their parent Service. The exact procedure varies between the Services.

Defence counsel tend to be civilian counsel with expertise in criminal law, instructed privately, by a firm of solicitors, or through the Armed Forces Criminal Legal Aid Authority (AFCLAA). Legal Aid funding is not available for minor cases involving administrative action, but if a serviceperson wishes to be represented by a lawyer the option to pay privately remains.

The Armed Forces Criminal Legal Aid Authority (AFCLAA) manages the provision of civilian criminal legal representation for all eligible service personnel and civilians, and advises on and executes policy. It is the single authority dealing with all aspects of criminal legal aid for those prosecuted through the SCJS. It is separate and independent from the Service Prosecuting Authority.

The court-martial consists of the Judge Advocate and either three or five lay members of the Board, who tend to sit on the Bench either side of the JA rather than in a jury box. Like juries, the goal is to find independent arbitrators. There are some notable differences, however, for example that a jury must have at least ten members whereas a Board is far smaller, and that the Board assists the JA both with finding of fact and with the sentencing exercise.

The composition of the court martial differs depending on whether the defendant is currently serving, is a civilian former-member of the Services, or is a civilian subject to Service jurisdiction.

For service personnel, the court-martial consists of a Judge Advocate and at least three or five members of the Board. The AFA 2006 provides for Boards comprising officers or warrant officers from all services. Officers are selected from outside the defendant's chain of command. The Board members are quite deliberately members of the military with an understanding of military life. Rather than a foreman selected from amongst themselves by the members of the jury, the President of the Board will be the most senior officer.

The composition is rather different for civilian defendants. If the civilian is ex-military being tried for offences committed whilst in service then the composition is entirely service personnel. If he faces offences committed as a civilian the board will be entirely civilian. In the case of multiple defendants, some service personnel and some civilians the board will be fully service personnel and some civilians. Where a case involves a civilian defendant, the court is known as the Service Civilian Court rather than the court-martial.

Like the Crown Court, there will be a PTPH, an arraignment and directions with the JA alone. The layout is entirely the same as a Crown Court although the conference facilities are usually vastly better. Video-link facilities are normally available to facilitate witness evidence and for client conferences, particularly useful for when you are based in the South East but your client is based in Scotland. Occasionally, prosecution counsel will appear by video link for administrative hearings and mentions.

The procedure at trial mirrors that of the Crown Court although members of the Board should be addressed as "Sir/Ma'am" and the

JA as "Your Honour". Civilian counsel wear wigs, gowns and business dress as normal, whereas prosecution counsel will wear military uniform. The Bar stands upon entry and exit of the JA and bows when service personnel salute. Be careful your wig does not fall off as this rather tends to mar the dignity of the court.

CHAPTER TWO
DISCIPLINARY OFFENCES

This Court Martial has wide jurisdiction to try any Service Offence. S50 AFA 2006 defines a "service offence". Also, any criminal conduct under the law of England and Wales is a Service offence by virtue of S42 AFA 2006.

This Chapter will consider in detail the most common offences the military practitioner is likely to encounter.

S8 Desertion

This offence is designed for those who are absent without leave on a period of active service. The points that must be proven are;

1. A person <u>subject to service law</u>
2. Is or remains <u>absent without leave</u> (which takes the meaning in S9)
3. <u>Intending</u> to avoid a period of active service

"Active service" is defined by S8(3) and includes actions or operations against an enemy, an operation outside the British Islands for the protection of life or property or the military occupation of a territory.

This offence is difficult to challenge and usually results in guilty pleas. It is only rarely possible to argue that there was any administrative miscommunication over when service personnel were due to return for duty. In cases where service personnel were <u>unable</u> to

return for duty it would be possible to argue that the intention was not to avoid active service.
This is a schedule 2 offence and so can only be tried by court martial.

Sentencing principles applicable to Desertion and AWOL

The same general principles apply to sentencing both cases of desertion and AWOL. Deterrence is a major factor to consider, but the court will also consider policy factors such as allowing for retraining.

Factors considered in determining sentence are the length of absence, impact on operational effectiveness, number of absences, the duty avoided, and the circumstances of both the departure and the return.

Often an attempt will be made to retain the offender in the Service. The offender loses their pay for the period of their absence, and the end of Service date will be extended to ensure that the absent days are still served. A sentence of detention without dismissal allows for retraining at the MCTC. If, on return to unit, it becomes clear that the retraining has been unsuccessful, the offender may then be discharged. Dismissal will only be awarded where it is justified in all the circumstances of the case.

Other relevant aggravating or mitigating factors may include:

i The circumstances under which the offender went absent

ii The effect of the absence on the unit, and the duty avoided

iii The length of absence

iv The number of separate absences

v Previous convictions for absence

vi Whether the absence ended in voluntary surrender or arrest, and whether arrest was resisted

vii Where the offender was during absence

viii Response to attempts by the Service to contact the offender

ix The offender's disciplinary and service record

x Any character references in his support

xi Any relevant medical or psychiatric evidence

Desertion is a more serious offence than AWOL. In assessing the seriousness of an offence of desertion, the court should also consider:

i Whether the accused went absent with the intention of avoiding active service [s 8(2)(b)] (the mischief being the adverse effect on operational effectiveness) rather than simply forming an intention to remain permanently absent [s 8(2)(a)], which constitute different forms of the offence of desertion

ii What service was actually avoided

iii The effect on his unit of his desertion

The maximum sentence for desertion with intent to avoid active service (s 8(2)(b)) is life imprisonment. The starting point is three years imprisonment and dismissal, with a range of one to four years imprisonment and detention if the sentence is under two years.

The maximum sentence for all other instances of desertion (s 8(2)(a)) is two years imprisonment. The starting point is eighteen months detention and dismissal.

S9 Absent without leave

The points that must be proven are;

1. A person subject to service law
2. Is intentionally or negligently absent without leave (S9(2)) or
3. He does an act, being reckless as to whether it will cause him to be AWOL and it does actually cause him to be AWOL (S9(3)).

The words of the statue make clear that an act includes an omission – S9(4).

"Negligently" is a specific service intent. Recklessness is a well known concept. It combines both a subjective and an objective standard. Negligence is a truly objective test measured against the yardstick of the reasonable man in the situation of the accused.

This is the most common offence before the Court Martial. It is very difficult to challenge and mostly leads to guilty pleas. The mens rea is neglect or intent. Therefore, all that need be proven is that the accused did something or failed to do something that a member of the armed forces ought not to do which can simply amount to failing to arrange his affairs so that he can report for duty.

The maximum sentence for being absent without leave is imprisonment for two years. The same general sentencing principles applied to cases of desertion, described above, also apply to AWOL.

The starting point for AWOL is 9 months detention if the offender is to be retained in the Service. If the offender is to be dismissed, the starting point is 6 months detention or a Service Community Order with unpaid work requirement. Any sentence of detention may be suspended if the court finds exceptional mitigating factors. The court should also consider whether a SSPO might be appropriate as an alternative to custody, especially in minor cases of AWOL or where the offender is required for pre-deployment training.

AWOL is regarded particularly seriously in the Royal Navy. The court will normally pass a slightly longer sentence on sailors, compared to soldiers and airmen, because of the detrimental effect on operational effectiveness if a sailor misses his ship.

S11. Misconduct towards a superior officer

S11(1)

1. A person subject to service law

2. Uses violence against a superior officer

3. He knows or has reasonable cause to believe that he is a superior officer

A strict interpretation of the statute would suggest it is one of strict liability. The only mens rea is to the belief in the rank of the witness. The offence does not even include the words "unlawfully" or "without reasonable excuse" which would exclude even private defence or the prevention of crime. Clearly there is a military need for subordination amongst the ranks but this may not survive a challenge under Article 6.

S11(2)

1. A person subject to service law

2. Uses behaviour towards a superior officer that is threatening or disrespectful and

3. He knows or has reasonable cause to believe that he is a superior officer

This subsection is wider than SS1 and is not limited to threats of violence – S11(3)(b). Indeed the communication need not even be in the presence of a superior officer if the communication is made to him – S11(3)(a). An intentional communication must be made however. An example would be using an agent to make such a communication.

The maximum sentence for using violence or threatening behaviour towards a superior officer (s 11(4)(a)) is imprisonment for 10 years. Where the injury is minor, the starting point is six months detention with a range of three to twelve months detention, and possible reduction in rank. Where the injury is significant, the starting point is two years' imprisonment with a range of one to four years, and dismissal. For threatening behaviour without violence the starting point is ninety days detention or SSPO.

The maximum sentence for using disrespectful behaviour towards a superior officer (s 11(4)(b)) is imprisonment for 2 years. The starting point is detention for 30 days or SSPO for 30 days.

Aggravating factors:

i deliberate malcontent

ii offence committed in front of those of inferior rank

iii flagrant contempt

iv offending while on operations

Mitigating factors:

i.i excitable immature youth

i.ii lack of appreciation of seriousness of actions or words

i.iii badly handled by superiors

i.iv disobedience occurs in a place remote from the Service context and does not undermine authority of the superior

i.v single instance not repeated

S12. Disobedience to lawful commands

iii. A person subject to service law

iv. Disobeys a lawful command and

v. He intends or is reckless as to whether he disobeys it

Service discipline is critical and misconduct is taken very seriously in order to ensure operational effectiveness.

When defending those charged with this offence it may be possible to challenge the lawfulness of the command. Conduct and commands alike must comply with service law, the criminal law of England and Wales, the law of armed conflict and the domestic law of the state in which they are operating.

The disobedience must be towards a "command" but that is defined very widely. It would include any lawful request made by a superior officer in a military capacity.

Mens rea may provide a defence to this charge. If the command lacked clarity either over the nature of the instruction or the time it should be acted upon then it might be possible to argue this was a genuine misunderstanding rather than an intentional or reckless disobedience. Also, if the command was such that it was impossible to perform; in Wisely, Rv Summary Appeal Court at Bulford, 2001, a Staff Sergeant had told the accused at 18.00hrs whilst he was intoxicated and in civilian clothes to parade outside the Guardsroom at 20.00hrs. The finding of the CO was appealed to the Deputy Judge Advocate who found that an order given in these circumstances could not be lawful because it was impossible.

The maximum sentence is imprisonment for 10 years. The starting point is reduction in rank and detention for 90 days within a range of 60 – 120 days. Reduction in rank and a short period of detention should always be considered, and in more serious cases dismissal should also be considered.

Aggravating factors:

- i deliberate malcontent
- ii offence committed in front of those of inferior rank
- iii flagrant contempt
- iv offending while on operations
- v disobedience created a security risk or put lives or safety of others in jeopardy

Mitigating factors:

- i.i excitable immature youth

i.ii lack of appreciation of seriousness of actions or words

i.iii badly handled by superiors

i.iv disobedience occurs in a place remote from the Service context and does not undermine authority of the superior

i.v single instance not repeated

S13. Contravention of standing orders

1. A person subject to service law
2. Contravenes a lawful order and
3. Knows or could reasonably be expected to know of the order

This section is used to capture disobedience with standing orders as opposed to disobedience to a specific command. The latter would fall under S12.

The standing order must have been published and the SPA must prove this and produce a copy. Common types of standing order breaches are being out of bounds, breaching the Royal Navy's "no touching rule" on ship, and driving offences.

The maximum sentence for breaching standing orders is imprisonment for two years. The starting point for a minor breach is a fine and/or a reprimand. For more serious offences, reduction in rank or forfeiture of seniority might be appropriate. The starting point for the most serious offences is detention with dismissal if appropriate. Out of bounds offences may be penalised by a short sentence of detention and/or reduction in rank. Minor breaches of the no touching rule may be penalised by detention and/or disrating or forfeiture of seniority. The most serious cases may result in dismissal.

S15. Failure to Perform a Duty and Negligent Performance of Duty

1. A person subject to service law commits an offence if

   a) Failing to attend for/perform duty

   b) Leaving a duty before permitted

   c) Failing to perform a duty

   d) Negligently performing a duty

This would cover, for instance, a soldier who oversleeps and is late for duty. Obviously this would not be appropriate for every instance but during a military deployment it could have very serious consequences and only a S15 charge would be appropriate.

The court should assess the seriousness of the failure or negligence by reference to the extent of the breach of duty, the age, training and experience of the offender, and the consequences of the breach. A common example of negligent performance of duty is a negligent discharge.

The maximum sentence is imprisonment for two years. The starting point for a minor breach is a fine and/or reprimand. Repeated minor breaches might result in a thirty-day SSPO. The starting point for more serious offences is a reduction in rank/loss of seniority and detention or SSPO for sixty or ninety days. The starting point for a negligent discharge involving no damage or injury and limited danger is a fine of between seven and fourteen days' pay.

Aggravating factors:

i seriousness of the breach of duty e.g. the conduct falls well below level expected of a competent and careful person of defendant's age, rank, experience and training

ii the negligence put safety or lives of others at risk

iii actual severe consequences, including injury or loss of life, or major loss of equipment or resources

iv poor professional record indicating a general lack of professionalism

v alcohol or drug induced conduct

vi horseplay or misuse of equipment

Mitigating factors:

i operational situation which reduces scope for exercising usual care and competence

ii isolated momentary lapse

iii extreme fatigue caused by long hours on duty

iv insufficient training

v minor consequences

vi no risk to safety or lives of others

vii conduct occurred during initial training on joining the Armed Forces (Phases 1 and 2)

viii youth and inexperience of offender

S19. Conduct prejudicial to good order and discipline

The points to be proven are

1. A person subject to service law
2. Does an act that is prejudicial to good order and service discipline
3. Intentionally or recklessly as to doing the act.
4. That the act was actually prejudicial to good order and service discipline

An act includes an omission – S19(2).

This offence has wide ambit and is open to abuse. It should not be used for conduct that amounts to an offence against any other section in the Act or a criminal offence in England and Wales as that would be covered by S42. A common example is sleeping on sentry duty. Potential prejudice is inadequate.

The SPA must prove both the conduct, the mens rea as to the conduct and that it caused prejudice. However, some conduct is likely to be so obviously harmful that it is prejudicial to service discipline; for instance in the case of Wilkinson 2000 WL 389652 where the driver to the then Air Vice-Marshall Bishop, the Chaplain-in-Chief to the RAF, took a car from the RAF station and drove to Manchester without authorisation and for his own purpose. He returned it the following day and so the matter could not be brought under S12 AFA as he lacked the intent permanently to deprive that would be required for theft.

The leading case is Dodman Case No : 97/3007/S2 1998, CMAC which was confirmed in the more recent case of Armstrong [2012] EWCA Crim 83. This case established that the mens rea is to the conduct which must be intentional or reckless.

The maximum sentence is imprisonment for two years.

The starting point for sleeping on watch or sentry duty is 120 days detention within a range of 28 to 180 days and reduction in rank.

Aggravating factors:

- i voluntary consumption of alcohol either while on watch or before duty
- ii duty is safety-critical
- iii sentry deliberately leaving his or her post
- iv sentry having made preparations to sleep, such as fetching a sleeping bag
- v potential danger caused by the sentry being asleep or leaving his or her post
- vi active theatre of operations and high existing security state

Mitigating factors:

- i no intention to sleep – but long hours worked on duty prior to offence
- ii duty is not safety critical
- iii offence committed during basic training

iv youth and inexperience of the offender

S20. Unfitness/misconduct through alcohol and drugs

1 A person subject to service law

2 Is unfit to be entrusted with his duty

3 Or any duty he might reasonably expected to be called upon to perform or

4 His behaviour is disorderly/likely to bring discredit to HM Forces

5 Due to the influence of alcohol or drugs

Duty

The JSP defines duty as the normal professional duties of service life. Those include but are not limited to;

- Any duty to attend a particular place
- Any duty imposed upon the accused because of their specific capacity, for instance mess treasure
- Any duty arising from some order
- Any duty arising from the accused's rank.

Unfit to be entrusted

This is tested objectively by superior officers in reliance upon the condition and behaviour of the accused rather than the amount of alcohol in his blood stream.

The accused need not be an extreme state of intoxication. The requirement is only that he is in a condition that renders him unfit to be entrusted.

But the alcohol or drugs must be such as to impair his ability to do his duty.

Drugs

This is not limited to controlled substances. It also includes any drug that affects control of the body.

It would exclude any medically prescribed drug if taken in accordance with advice.

Likely to bring discredit

The Pt1 of the MSL defines this at 1-7-65.

Whether conduct is “likely to bring discredit” is determined as “behaviour that falls below the standard that is expected” of Service personnel.

The misconduct must occur in a location where the public are likely to witness it and they must be aware that the accused is a service person.

The maximum sentence is two years’ imprisonment. For minor offences the starting point is a fine of ten days’ pay, within a range of seven to fourteen days’ pay and a reprimand or severe reprimand if applicable to the offender’s rank. For offences of medium seriousness the starting point is a reduction in rank, a short period of detention or SSPO. For major offences the starting point is 120 days’ detention, with a range of 30 to 180 days. The court may sentence repeat offenders to dismissal.

Aggravating factors:

- i on duty, unable to perform a specific duty
- ii on board a ship at sea or aircraft in flight
- iii at an official function
- iv in the public eye
- v put at risk the safety of others
- vi injury to others
- vii under age
- viii alcoholism where the offender has ignored help after diagnosis

Mitigating factors:

- i offence committed in Service Club or in Single Living Accommodation
- ii no disturbance and placid behaviour
- iii off duty
- iv caused by welfare or personal problems

S21. Fighting or threatening behaviour

The points that must be proven are;

S21(1)

1. A person subject to service law commits an offence if
2. Without reasonable excuse
3. He fights another person

S21(2)

1. Without reasonable excuse
2. His behaviour is threatening, abusive, insulting or provocative.

A person's behaviour includes anything said by him – S21(3).

This often serves as a lesser alternative to public order offences such as affray, violent disorder or riot brought under S42 Criminal Conduct. Contrary to common view, fighting is not easier for the SPA to prove. The inclusion of the words "without reasonable excuse" would include the civilian defence of private defence although the evidential burden shifts to the defence in service law.

It is important to remember that there is no requirement for the fighting or behaviour to take place in a public place as the Public Order Act requires.

The offence of fighting is distinct from the offence of assault. Fighting requires more than a one-sided attack.

The starting point for minor offences that do not cause injury, alarm or distress is a fine of 21 days' pay within a range of 14 to 28 days pay and a reprimand or a severe reprimand if applicable to the offender's rank. The maximum sentence for fighting is two years' imprisonment. Because fighting requires the involvement of more than one person engaged in a fight, service compensation orders are rarely appropriate and the degree of personal injury resulting is not a weighty consideration. For offences that are more than minor the starting point is reduction in rank or 90 days' detention, with a range of 30 to 180 days.

S22. Ill-treatment of Subordinates

This section provides

1. An <u>officer, warrant officer or NCO</u> who
2. <u>Ill treats</u>
3. A <u>subordinate</u>
4. <u>Subject to service law</u>
5. <u>Intending</u> or being <u>reckless</u> as to whether he is ill treating
6. And <u>knows</u> or has <u>reasonable cause to know</u> that he is a subordinate

This is designed to address initiation ceremonies. Assault charges remain more appropriate for specific acts of violence.

Ill treatment is not defined in the act. It is left as a question of fact for the Board and includes a wide range of behaviours which perhaps was the intention of those who legislate. The MSL includes the following entry

> *"Ill treatment is to be given its normal dictionary meaning of treating badly or cruelly. A series of minor actions against a victim, which would in themselves amount to offences of assault, might amount to ill treatment. ill-treatment includes but is not limited to physical Force. bullying or frightening may suffice as no behaviour or treatment design necessarily harsh or which degrades or humiliates another person"*

In the case of Ireland v UK [1978] ECHR 1 it was found that "ill treatment must attain a minimum level of Severity if it is to fall within Article 3. The assessment of this Minimum is, in the nature of things, relative"

The maximum sentence is two years' imprisonment. The starting point for most cases is reduction in rank and 9 months detention, with a range of 6 to 12 months. The most serious cases can result in dismissal.

Aggravating factors:

- i conduct over a protracted period
- ii conduct undertaken in concert with others
- iii physical or severe mental abuse
- iv mental or physical injury to victim or harm to victim's career
- v abuse of trainees in basic training
- vi forcing victims to undertake demeaning or disgraceful conduct

vii abuse of rank to obtain financial benefit

viii racial or sexual element

ix large rank disparity between offender and victim

Mitigating factors:

i one-off incident of a minor nature

ii over-zealous attempt to reinforce training

iii no injury to victim

iv genuine remorse and apology to victim

S23. Disgraceful conduct of a cruel or indecent kind

1 A person <u>subject to service law</u>

2 <u>Does an act</u>

3 Which is <u>cruel or indecent</u>

4 And is <u>disgraceful</u>

Terms like "cruel" and "indecent" are given their normal English meaning. The section is worded disjunctively. Therefore the charge may be either of "cruel" or "indecent" conduct.

There is clearly overlap between words such as "cruel/indecent" and "disgraceful" but it is important to understand that the SPA must prove the conduct was both cruel or indecent and disgraceful. Indecent conduct in particular may be rendered disgraceful because it takes place in a public place even though it would not be in private place.

This charge would be available to deal with initiation ceremonies although the leading cases have been varied.

In Lee [2005] All ER the accused kicked a dog causing him to die. He was charged with disgraceful conduct of a cruel kind contrary to S66 Army Act 1955.

The starting point for most cases is reduction to the ranks and 9 months detention, with a range of 6 to 12 months detention. Very minor offences can take the starting point of an SSPO, but serious cases can result in dismissal in addition to any sentence of detention. The maximum available sentence is imprisonment for 2 years

Aggravating factors:

i abuse of position of authority

ii in public or in front of a group

iii racial or sadomasochistic element

iv other factors relating to ill treatment

Mitigating factors:

i one-off incident of a minor nature

ii overzealous attempt to reinforce training

iii no injury to victim

iv genuine remorse and apology to victim

S42. Criminal Conduct

The points that must be proven are;

1. A person subject to service law
2. Does an act that would be an offence in England or Wales

It is important to note that this offence applies outside of the jurisdiction. This also can be used regardless of the existence of another appropriate service offence.

There are also offences of attempting criminal conduct (S43), conspiring to commit criminal conduct (S44) and the remaining inchoate offences (S46-47).

For relevant sentencing considerations please refer to the specific criminal conduct offences in the next chapter.

CHAPTER THREE
CRIMINAL CONDUCT OFFENCES

Criminal practitioners will already be very familiar with the various criminal conduct offences. This book will not rehearse the elements of those offences here, but rather will set out the Service-specific sentencing considerations for each category of offence, as set out in the Guidance on Sentencing in the Court Martial which is considered at sentence alongside any Sentencing Council guidelines.

Serious offences

Serious offences such as homicide, rape, and armed robbery are sentenced as they would be in the Crown Court. Occasionally there might be mitigating factors arising from Service-specific factors such as PTSD suffered on operations, that would allow the court to impose a lower sentence. To the contrary, serious drugs offences might be sentenced more harshly than in the Crown Court due to the Service-wide policies against drug use, and the highly damaging impact of drug use on unit cohesion.

Drug offences

The Armed Forces take drug abuse particularly seriously, for clear and obvious reasons. The nature of military service is inherently dangerous and is therefore correspondingly disciplined. The effects of drug use on an individual's judgment, health, fitness, reliability, general performance, and interpersonal relationships can be devastating in any context. Teamwork and unit cohesion is also of high importance in the military. Where the individual is expected to carry weapons, use dangerous equipment, and safeguard the safety of civilians and colleagues, the risks of drug abuse are even greater.

Joint Service Publication (JSP) 835 sets out the Armed Forces' policy on drug abuse. In essence, misuse of drugs poses a significant threat to operational effectiveness and is incompatible with service life. With this in mind, regardless of any criminal sanction imposed for a drugs offence, the defendant must be dismissed and reduced in rank (if appropriate) unless it is not in the service interests to do so. Only in exceptional circumstances will any member of the Armed Forces be retained following drug misuse.

The starting point for possession of drugs is dismissal with 90 days' custody, with a range from dismissal to dismissal with 180 days' custody. The Sentencing Council guidelines are unlikely to be deemed sufficient or applicable in the Service context given the considerations outlined above.

Aggravating factors:

i. Quantity other than very small

ii. Use within the Service environment or on duty

iii. Previous conviction for drugs offences

iv. Corruption of others

v. Abuse of position of authority (in supply cases)

vi. Class A drugs

Mitigating factors:

i. very small quantity

ii. youthful first-time experimentation

iii. social setting away from the Service environment

iv. youth of offender

v. admission of involvement at early stage

vi. genuine remorse

vii. co-operation with investigators

viii. special personal or domestic circumstances

Exceptionally an offender may be retained in the Service if the Court Martial finds the following factors in his favour:

i. the offender was young and inexperienced

ii. it was a first offence involving singular use on one occasion

iii. the chances of reform are good

iv. the offender expresses remorse

v. the offender has significant potential

vi. it is in the interest of the Service to retain the offender

Offences of dishonesty

Dishonesty is not consistent with service in the Armed Forces because it is corrosive to unit cohesiveness and morale.

Serious aggravation will be found where there is a breach of trust or the theft or dishonesty offence is against the employer. The same considerations should apply as in the civilian courts, although greater aggravation may be found for offences within the Service context.

The sentencing court will consider the following factors:

1. The rank of the offender
2. the degree of trust reposed
3. the value involved
4. the effects of the lost items on operational effectiveness
5. the period of time over which the offences have been committed.

The starting point for offences of dishonesty is dismissal, as would be the case for any other employer. As a rule, the court should not impose a sentence of imprisonment if the level of culpability would not justify a prison sentence in the civilian system. However, a higher standard of honesty and integrity is expected of members of the Armed Forces, so a sentence of detention might be appropriate. The rank of the offender is particularly relevant to culpability; ordinarily a commissioned officer would expect to be dismissed even for a first offence.

The court will find great aggravation in the type of theft known as 'barrack room' or 'mess deck' thefts, that is, when an individual steals items from their colleagues. This is of importance because service personnel may live in very close quarters which requires a higher level of mutual respect. For barrack room theft, the starting point is dismissal and 6 months custody, and a range of 3 to 9 months detention.

A common type of Service-fraud is JPA fraud. JPA is the online system whereby service personnel can register claims for expenses such as travel and subsistence. Only a small number of claims are audited so it is possible to make false claims, whether frequent minor "exaggerations" of expenses actually incurred, or entirely fictional claims. When it comes to mitigating offences of JPA fraud, mitigation based on factors such as peer pressure, small sums, opportunistic claims, or the assertion that such offending is tolerated will carry little weight.

For JPA fraud, the court should consider the value and number of fraudulent transactions to establish the starting point. For three or fewer separate frauds and/or a total amount of less than £500, the starting point is 6 months' detention. For cases involving four or more separate frauds, the starting point is dismissal. Any period of detention depends on the value of the frauds:

- £500 – £2000: SP of 6 months detention or Service Community Order
- £2000 – £10,000: SP of 12 months detention
- Over £10,000: The court should apply Sentencing Council guidelines

<u>Offences of violence</u>

Violent offending by members of the Armed Forces often attract deterrent sentences, especially where they have been committed under the influence of alcohol. This is because service personnel are trained to exercise controlled aggression and lawful violence towards the enemy, which requires a high degree of discipline. Criminal violence displays a lack of discipline which can undermine operational effectiveness and cohesion, especially when the victim is another member of the Armed Forces.

The starting points for more serious offences of violence, that is, grievous bodily harm under s.18 and s.20 OAPA 1861, are those provided in the Sentencing Council guidelines. Where this level of violence is directed at superiors, or is an abuse of rank or authority, the aggravation may justify heavier sentences than set out in the guidelines, but factors resulting from operational considerations may amount to mitigation justifying a lower sentence.

Offences of ABH are very common in the Service context. Where the injuries sustained are serious or permanent, the court should consider dismissal or reduction in rank. Similarly, if the defendant serves in a particular role such as the Service Police, it may be inappropriate for them to continue serving in that role post-conviction. Custody should be considered in all cases.

Starting points within the Sentencing Council Guideline for ABH may be adjusted as follows:

- Category 1: 18 months custody within a range of 1 – 3 years
- Category 2: 9 months custody within a range of 6 – 18 months
- Category 3: 120 days custody within a range of 90 – 180 days

General aggravating and mitigating factors for violent offences are set out below.

Aggravating factors:

i. harassment including bullying and abuse of rank

ii. group action, particularly in cases of bullying

iii. insubordination

iv. vulnerability of the victim, for example, in the victim's own home

v. drunkenness

vi. violence against citizens of host countries

Mitigating factors:

i. Stress and Post-Traumatic Stress Disorder

ii. Impulsive action or provocation in an operational context

Sexual offences

As in the civilian courts, only judges who are ticketed to deal with serious sexual offences are allowed to sit in such cases.

For serious sexual offences, the starting points are those within the Sentencing Council guidelines, but there may be additional aggravating factors associated with the Services which should be taken into account. Dismissal or dismissal with disgrace is almost inevitable apart from in the most exceptional cases.

General aggravating factors for sexual offences include:

i. a difference in rank and/or age between the offender and the victim, or the abuse of a position of authority (especially where grooming is involved)

ii. damage to the reputation of the armed forces

iii. the impact on future employability of the offender within the service

Sexual offending involving indecent images is often incompatible with their continued service in the Armed Forces, for example due to the need to work with young people.

For offences involving indecent images, offenders should be dismissed unless there are exceptional reasons for retention in the Service. This is in addition to any sentence based on the Sentencing Council guidelines. The judge may consider it necessary for the board members to view the relevant images, but this is a matter for judicial discretion.

Sexual assaults are normally more serious in a Service context than in civilian life because they can cause resentment and undermine unit cohesion, with offenders often being ostracised by their peers. Normally the sentencing court will consider a short period of custody to be appropriate for even the most minor offences, and reduction in rank is almost inevitable.

The same notification requirements for persons convicted of sexual offences apply in the Courts Martial as in the civilian courts, namely those set out in Part 2 of the Sexual Offences Act 2003. These requirements are an automatic consequence of conviction and sentence, and are not part of the sentence as such. It is open to the court to impose a Sexual Harm Prevention Order with appropriate terms. The MCTC does not have the facilities to provide Sexual Offence Treatment Programmes (SOTPs) so these should not be imposed in conjunction with detention.

Motoring offences

Motoring offences on military establishments are subject to a different sentencing regime than in the civilian courts, because the Court Martial has no power to impose penalty points or disqualification from driving. Driving offences are often charged as breaches of standing orders.

For motoring offences committed overseas, the offender's CO can withdraw the military-issued driving permit required under Standing Orders to drive overseas, following administrative rather than disciplinary action. These permits are not driving licences, but are issued to an individual upon completion of training and written tests. Withdrawal of the permit prevents a service person from driving in that country, although it has no effect on their UK driving licence.

Sentences for serious driving offences such as dangerous driving, causing death by careless or dangerous driving, and drink driving should be based on the Sentencing Council guidelines, along with dismissal in cases that result in imprisonment.

The starting point for speeding, careless driving and other minor offences is a fine of 5 days' pay and a recommendation for the withdrawal of military driving permit by the offender's CO.

The starting point for drink driving depends on how far over the limit the offender was. Where the level of alcohol is under twice the limit the starting point is a fine of 28 days' pay. Where the level of alcohol is over twice the limit, the starting point is 90 days detention.

Firearms/ammunition offences

Members of the Armed Forces are expected to display exemplary behaviour when it comes to handling firearms and ammunition. Service Personnel are subject to the same laws as civilians when it comes to being in possession of firearms and ammunition when not on duty, including the rules in relation to trophies of war and the requirements for decommissioned weapons.

When sentencing firearms offences, the court should refer to Current Sentencing Practice and applicable Sentencing Council guidelines. In addition, there is a presumption of dismissal except in truly exceptional circumstances.

The mandatory minimum sentence of 5 years set out in s51A of the Firearms Act 1968 applies to relevant offences under s.5. The court has the discretion to find exceptional circumstances and impose a lower sentence. The reasons for any departure from the minimum sentence should be clearly specified in the sentencing remarks.

In *R v Nightingale* [2013] the trial judge listed the following exceptional circumstances which were accepted by the Court of Appeal in dismissing Nightingale's appeal against a suspended sentence of 2 years detention:

i. He was an exceptional soldier who had served with distinction in the SAS including on operations;

ii. He had done more than his duty by improving the medical care of those who receive traumatic injury by developing the Nightingale dressing;

iii. He suffered a brain injury in 2009 resulting in some mental impairment which may have affected the way he failed to decommission the pistol or return the ammunition;

iv. He dealt with weapons routinely both at home and abroad and was required to be expert with them. The court accepted that weapons were a normal part of his life and he would not have held them in the sort of awe which civilians would.

v. He had no criminal intention – his offending was because of poor administrative practices and possibly forgetfulness.

CHAPTER FOUR
PRE-TRIAL MATTERS

This chapter will address matters including police powers, investigations, arrest, interview, and preliminary hearings.

Police Powers

Arrest

Investigations and evidence gathering is carried out by the Service police.

Broadly, the Military Police have comparable powers to the civilian police though there are some differences. The Service police can make arrests and use force under S67 AFA 2006. The rights of others to make arrests are far more complicated than in civilian life and arise more commonly. Not everybody subject to service law can arrest any other person subject to service law. Power of arrests are to be found in part 3 of AFA 2006, S67 – S97.

S67 sets out the powers of arrest.

An officer may only be arrested by a person of superior rank unless he is engaged in a mutiny, quarrel or disorder and then by an officer of any rank, a Service police officer or a provost officer or his agent – S67(2) AFA 2006.

A soldier may be arrested by officer, non commissioned officer of superior rank, a service policeman or a provost officer alike – S67(3) AFA 2006

A civilian subject to service discipline may be arrested by an officer, a service police NCO or a provost officer – S67(4) AFA 2006.

Further the power of arrest can be transferred from the person in whom it is vested to anybody that he orders to make arrests – S67(6) AFA 2006

The introduction of the AFA 2006 also impacted upon "bail". Before the Act, bail was a decision for the commanding officer. Now, a suspect must be produced before the JA and his continued detention must be considered subject to S111 AFA 2006.

The civilian police do have powers to arrest for a service offence but only a warrant is ordered by the JA – S313. That would be upon the application of a service policeman, a CO or the SPA. Once the warrant is executed though the SP must be returned to service custody as soon as practicable – S313(4) AFA 2006.

Only in the case of desertion or AWOL can a SP be arrested by civilian police without a warrant – S314 AFA 2006. He must either be placed before the next available magistrates court or transferred to service custody or release subject to a condition that he reports to service custody – S315 AFA 2006.

Similarly the magistrates when dealing with an absentee or deserter must transfer him into service custody or release him subject to a reporting condition – S317 AFA 2006

Under S111 AFA 2006 the Judge Advocate can also direct that a person be arrested as long as he has been arraigned and taking him into custody is justified. Whether or not it is justified is decided upon the same factors as the civilian bail act considers – fear of commission of further offences, failing to surrender or interference with witnesses.

AFA 2006 allows for the arrest and detention of service personnel by the civilian authorities in the following circumstances

- S313 – under a warrant issued by a judge advocate
- S314 – absentees and deserters found at large
- S3115 – absentees and deserters who hand themselves into the civilian police
- S316 – proceedings before a civilian court where a person is suspected of absenteeism
- S317 – on a warrant for the arrest of a person released under S315, 316 or 317
- S318 – arrest of a person unlawfully at large

Powers of stop and search and broadly similar to those of the civilian police but they are extended to other personnel.

A service policeman has the power to stop and search any person subject to service discipline and any vehicle in their charge in certain circumstances – S75 AFA 2006.

The circumstances are that service policeman have reasonable grounds to suspect that the search will reveal stolen or prohibited items, but the search for reveal service stores unlawfully obtained or that the search will reveal a controlled drug.

These powers can only be exercised in specified places. A full list of the locations can be found at S78 AFA 2006 but, in effect, the service policeman can exercise the power to stop and search anywhere on private premises which includes service living accommodation.

A CO or other Officer can authorise service personnel under his command to exercise the power of stop and search in the same place as a service policeman – S76 AFA 2006. it is fair to say that this is considered exceptional and should only really be used in relation to a specific person however.

Search

Search powers are governed by the Armed Forces (Power of Stop and Search, Search, Seizure and Retention) Order 2009. These powers largely mirror those of the civilian police.

The service police may search any person who is arrested where there are reasonable grounds to believe that he may be a danger to himself or others, has concealed anything upon him or has something that may be used to escape from service custody – S70 AFA 2006.

Any person who is exercising a power under S67 AFA may search the arrested person if he has reasonable grounds to believe that he may present a danger to himself or others.

With the authority of the arrested person's commanding officer, the arrested person may be searched if there are reasonable grounds to believe that the arrested person would escape from service custody or conceal, damage, alter or destroy evidence – S71(2).

The CO can only instigate such a search if the assistance of a service or civilian police officer cannot be obtained, or that it would lead to a delay allowing the arrested person to escape or dispose of evidence – S71(3)

The persons authorised to search must provide the arrested person with his name, rank, unit and authority for the search and its objective – Art 5 of AF(PSSSSR)O 2009.

Stop and search

The Service police have power to stop and search persons and vehicles under S75 AFA 2006.

A service police officer may search any person if there are reasonable grounds for believing he is subject to service law or a civilian subject to service discipline – S75(1)(a) AFA 2006.

A service vehicle may also be searched if such a person is in charge of it – S75(1)(b) AFA 2006.

Any other vehicle may be searched if there are reasonable grounds to believe it is in the charge of such a person – S75(1)(c). Anything found in such a vehicle may be searched under S75(1)(d) AFA 2006.

For any search to be lawful under S75(2) AFA 2006 there must be reasonable grounds for suspecting:

1. That the search will reveal stolen or prohibited items
2. That it will reveal Her Majesty's stores have been unlawfully obtained
3. That a person is in possession of a controlled drug

4. That a search of the vehicle will reveal a controlled drug

Any search does not have to be conducted by service police. A search may be conducted by any person subject to service law if authorised by an officer and in a location permitted by S78 – S76 AFA 2006.

There must be reasonable grounds to believe that the search will reveal stolen articles, controlled drugs or Her Majesty's stores – S76(1) AFA 2006.

Such a person has power to detain a person or vehicle for the purposes of such a search (S76(1)(b)) and to seize any article that is discovered of relevance (S76(1)(c)).

Searches under S75 and 76 may be exercised only in a place permitted under S78 AFA 2006. Those are:

1. Any place to which the public has access
2. Any place to which people have ready access but are not a dwelling or service living accommodation
3. Any premises which is not service living accommodation

<u>Bail and custody</u>

It is important to understand that the service police have no power to grant bail. Bail is entirely under the control of the JAG and governed by Part 4 of AFA 2006 and the Armed Forces (Custody Proceedings) Rules 2009.

Save for arrest authorised by the CO under S99-102 a person subject to service law cannot be held in service custody without being charged.

Custody without charge – ss 98-104

S67 is clear. Save for the provisions of S99-102, no person may be kept in service custody pre charge.

Custody hearings are governed by two principle sections; pre charge by S98-104 AFA 2006 and after charge by S105-109 AFA 2006/ Armed Forces (Custody Proceedings) Rules 2009.

When a person is arrested under S67, S99 imposes an obligation upon those responsible for the arrest to report it and the grounds for detention to the CO of the arrested person as soon as "practicable".

If the CO has reasonable grounds to believe that keeping him in custody without charge is necessary to preserve or obtain evidence and that the investigation is being conducted diligently and expeditiously then he may authorise the keeping of that person in service custody – S99(4) AFA 2006. A CO may authorise detention for up to 48 hours – S99(6) AFA 2006.

S100 AFA demands that the decision to keep a person in service custody is reviewed by his CO at 12-hour intervals.

After the expiry of 48 hours, a detained person must be released unless further detention is authorised by the judge advocate up to a maximum of 96 hours – S101 AFA 2006. Where it is not practicable for this to be done by the judge advocate, a CO may authorise continued detention. This rarely arises now that judge advocates are available by remote means.

After 96 hours, a detained person must be charged or released.

Custody after charge

Once service personnel are charged, they will generally be released.

If a CO wants to retain an accused person in custody then he must be brought before the judge advocate as soon as practicable – S105(1) AFA 2006.

The judge advocate can order detention in service custody for up to 8 days (S105 AFA 2006) if satisfied of any of the following criteria;

1. there are substantial grounds to believe the suspect would fail to attend any hearing, commit further offences or interfere with witness/obstruct justice.
2. The accused should be detained for his own protection
3. Insufficient information has been obtained to make a decision in relation to 1 & 2.
4. It would be impracticable to complete enquiries without keeping the accused in service custody.

The judge advocate must take into account the nature and seriousness of the offence, the character, antecedents and social ties of the accused, the strength of the evidence and other relevant factor – S105(4) AFA 2006.

Bail conditions

Bail conditions do not exist in a service context. However, the judge advocate may release an accused person from service custody on "requirements".

Requirements can be any that the judge advocate deem necessary. Commonly they include residing at a particular place, not to leave the barracks, reporting at the unit guard house. Non contact requirements are difficult to comply with in a service context especially if the witnesses are other service personnel.

Requirements must be needed to ensure that the accused person attends proceedings, does not commit further offences or obstruct justice.

In the event that custody is authorised by a judge advocate, a CO retains a duty to consider whether custody remains necessary. This duty is ongoing – S108.

A judge advocate must further review the need for detention within 8 days of the first decision. Custody must be reviewed at 8-day intervals unless the detained person consents to a longer period of detention.

Custody is rarer in the service context.

Preliminary hearings

PTPH and Goodyear

The most common preliminary hearing is the PTPH. They mirror largely the civilian system. They are conducted by the JA sitting alone. Arraignment and casement takes place therein.

Despite the fact that sentencing is conducted by lay members and the Judge together, a Goodyear indication may be sought from the judge before pleas are entered at any preliminary hearing. The advantage of this is that the indication would bind the lay members of the panel at the time of sentence.

Public interest

When making representations to the SPA at PTPH or any earlier hearing, bear in mind that the public interest test is slightly different within the military setting. A prosecutor must consider whether a case passes the evidential test before applying the public interest consideration. If the case does pass that test then a prosecutor must consider if a prosecution is needed "in the public, including Service, interest."

What is the "service interest" can be determined with reference to the Manual of Service Law, Volume 1. This refers to whether "disciplinary action is consistent with justice and with the fair and efficient maintenance of discipline and operational effectiveness, and whether there are Service factors that make disciplinary action inappropriate". It is important to note that the "service interest" is subsumed within the public interest and can never over ride it. However, factors such as provocation from other service personnel are given far more weight than in the civilian courts.

Defendant's Assisting Officer

Service personnel have the opportunity to nominate a Defendant's Assisting Officer (DAO) to help them prepare their case.

The DAO is a serving officer. Their position is a purely administrative one but he can be very useful especially in cases where counsel is instructed directly by AFLAA. They can be tasked with ensuring that the defendant obtains the evidence for which he is asked.

The DAO is not legally qualified. They have no rights of audience or right to speak on the defendant's behalf at all. However, they are bound by confidentiality – MSL, Volume 2, Annex B.

CHAPTER FIVE
TRIAL

Jurisdiction

The Court Martial has jurisdiction to try all criminal offences under the law of England and Wales by virtue of the Armed Forces Act 2006 s 42. Within the Service jurisdiction these offences are known as "criminal conduct offences". Persons who are either subject to Service law or civilians subject to Service discipline may be tried in the Court Martial for criminal conduct offences. A limited number of criminal conduct offences (listed in Schedule 1 of the Act) may be heard summarily by the Commanding Officer but only if the defendant is a person subject to Service law.

S50 Armed Forces Act 2006 provides the Court Martial with the jurisdiction to try any service offence including those committed outside the UK. For misconduct within the UK, there may be an overlap with civilian authorities although the civilian authorities have primary jurisdiction. The more serious the offence, the greater the reluctance to leave the matter to the Court Martial.

A person tried in the military courts cannot face further proceedings in the civilian courts and vice versa – S63 Armed Forces Act 2006.

Evidence

The civilian rules of evidence apply to military court martials unless they have been disapplied or modified by other enactments – Rule 73(1) Armed Forces Court Martial Rules 2009 (hereafter AF (CM) R 2009).

R75 AF (CM) 2009 allows for proof by written statement.

R76 AF (CM) 2009 provides for S10 admissions

R77 AF (CM) 2009 allows for use of documents to refresh memory.

R78-80 AF (CM) 2009 covers bad character.

R81-82 AF (CM) 2009 covers hearsay.

R83 AF (CM) 2009 allows for evidence of enlistment. Evidence of enlistment will be relevant to any case where there is a need to show that a person is subject to service discipline. This is usually no more than the enlistment papers.

R84 AF (CM) 2009 covers evidence of service. This covers dates of service, any discharge, ranks attained, transfers, any suspensions in rank or entitlement to wear decoration.

Service record is admissible under R85. These must be made under any Act or Queen's Regulations.

Expert evidence may be admitted with leave of the judge under R88 AF(CM) 2009.

Special measures may be used under R89-100 AF (CM) 2009. They are used less frequently than in the civilian courts save for the power of live link. This is used liberally largely to allow for operational effectiveness as personnel need not be taken from their international duties in order to give evidence before the Court Martial. The JA has a power in addition to those under R89-100 to order that any person may attend any proceedings by live link. If in service custody such persons must attend by live link – r18 SCC Rules and rule 18 AF (CM) R 2009.

Submissions of no case to answer may be made under R104 AF (CM) R 2009.

Trial procedure

The military trial procedure largely mirrors the civilian one. There are some differences.

The SPA present their case first, followed by the defence case.

At the conclusion the JA sums up to the lay members and they retire to consider the evidence. Further directions can be sought from the JA but they must be given in open court – R109 AF (CM) R 2009. The votes of the lay members are given in reverse order of seniority in order to avoid pressure from more senior members upon others. The findings are announced by the President in open court.

Under R110 AF (CM) R 2009 the JA has powers in relation to the findings of the Board that do have an equivalent in the criminal courts. Under R101(3) the JA, if satisfied the findings are "acceptable in law" shall sign a record of the findings. Under R101(4) if not so satisfied he shall direct the lay members to withdraw and reconsider. Since the JA plays no part in the deliberation of the Board it is difficult to envisage how this could be exercised.

There is also a power under to convict of an offence other than that charged. Under S161 Armed Forces Act 2006 the Court Martial may, if they acquit of the offence that was charged, convict of another service offence if the allegations in the charge sheet amount to an allegation of that offence. A similar power exists in relation to the civilians under S281 AFA 2006.

CHAPTER SIX
INTRODUCTION TO SENTENCE

Sentencing in the court martial largely mirrors sentencing in the civilian jurisdiction. There is parity between sentencing in the SCJS and the civilian justice system in that most of the sentencing options introduced by the Criminal Justice Act 2003 are available to the SCJS, and maximum terms apply equally. Similarly, the court martial will have regard to Sentencing Guidelines and to Court of Appeal judgments.

Sentencing Methodology

The sentencing court will work through the following steps when considering sentence:

1. Refer to any relevant Sentencing Council guidance including sentencing guidelines

2. Place the offence in the appropriate category

3. Apply any aggravating/mitigating factors in the sentencing guideline

4. Consider imposing a sentence of detention rather than a community penalty if the offender is not to be dismissed

5. Apply any additional Service features which may justify a departure from that sentence e.g. reduction in rank, dis-missal, and adjust sentence accordingly

6. Apply the appropriate credit for an early guilty plea

The Court Martial has the discretion to apply whatever punishment is just, appropriate and lawful, but suggested starting points do exist. These are set out in [Annex 1] at the back of this book. The starting points are those suggested by the [name of the guide] and are based on the sentencing of a first-time offender on conviction after a plea of not guilty, and taking account of Sentencing Council guidelines.

Due consideration should be given to unique Service features. For example, a higher sentence may be justified where the offence is potentially damaging to Service discipline, such as when a soldier assaults a superior officer or steals from his peers. An offender's rank will be very relevant to culpability, with higher ranks likely to be held more culpable for their actions. Other features, such as loss of pension rights or matters arising from operational duties, may afford some mitigation and lead to a more lenient sentence.

The sentencing judge is obliged to state in open court the reasons for deciding on the sentence passed. The reasons must be given in ordinary language and general terms so that the offender can understand the effect of the sentence (s.252(1)). Where the starting point is departed from, the judge should address this in the reasons.

The Court Martial must have regard to the principle of totality in considering sentence, and in considering whether to impose consecutive or concurrent sentences for multiple offences. The court is required to pass a separate sentence in respect of each offence (s.255).

Available sentences and other orders

There are sentences available to the court martial that do not exist in the civilian courts, such as dismissal and service detention, specific to the military environment, addressed in detail below. The available sentences under s.164 are:

i. Imprisonment (including custody for young offenders)

ii. Dismissal with disgrace from Her Majesty's Service

iii. Dismissal from Her Majesty's Service

iv. Detention for a term not exceeding two years

v. Forfeiture of a specified term of seniority or all seniority

vi. Reduction in rank or disrating

vii. Financial penalty

viii. Service community order

ix. Severe reprimand or reprimand

x. Service supervision and punishment order

xi. Minor punishments:

    a. stoppage of leave

    b. restrictions of privileges

    c. admonition

xii. Service compensation order.

In addition the Court Martial may impose any of the following Orders:

i. Hospital Order [s 169(2)]

ii. Service Supervision Order [s 170]

iii. Overseas Community Order [s 182] – civilians only

iv. Conditional Discharge [s 185] – civilians only

v. Suspended Sentence Order [s 200]

vi. Sexual Harm Prevention Order [s232A and Sexual Offences Act 2003 s 137(2)]

vii. Service Restraining Order [s 229]

viii. Financial Penalty Enforcement Order [s 322]

Pre-Sentence and Psychiatric Reports

As in the civilian criminal justice system, pre-sentence reports exist in the SCJS to assist the court in deciding on the appropriate sentence for a particular offender.

Under s.256(1), the court must obtain and consider a pre-sentence report before passing certain sentences unless it is of the opinion that it is unnecessary to do so. These sentences are:

i. Imprisonment

ii. Detention

iii. Dismissal/dismissal with disgrace

iv. A community sentence

v. A sentence in respect of a dangerous offender; or

vi. A sentence in respect of violent or sexual offences.

The court must obtain and consider a medical report before passing a custodial sentence on an offender who is or appears to be mentally disordered (s 258).

CHAPTER SEVEN
SENTENCES AVAILABLE

Imprisonment and Service Detention

The same sentencing considerations taken into account in the civilian court will apply in the court martial. Sentences of imprisonment may be suspended by the court martial, and existing suspended sentences may be activated or varied. The court may attach community requirements to a suspended sentence but would not normally do so unless the offender was also sentenced to dismissal. Where a WO or NCO is sentenced to imprisonment, they are also reduced to the lowest rank that can be awarded by the court martial.

Service detention involves deprivation of liberty but is nevertheless a less serious sentence than imprisonment and focuses on rehabilitation rather than punishment, so would not normally be an appropriate sentence for the more serious offences. Although it does not carry the same stigma as imprisonment, a detainee serving a sentence of service detention will not receive any salary for the duration of their detention, and time served does not count towards pension entitlements, for example.

Service detention is only available for those of Warrant Officer rank and below. The maximum period of service detention that can be imposed is two years.

Service detention of between 14 days and two years are served at the Colchester-based Military Corrective Training Centre, or MCTC. The MCTC can house up to 264 servicemen and women from all three branches of the armed forces, in accordance with the provisions of the Service Custody and Service of Relevant Sentences Rules 2009 (SCSRSR 09). This includes Detainees Under Sentence (DUS), and Detainees Not Under Sentence (DNUS), that is, those on remand.

There are two categories of Detainees Under Sentence, namely those who are to remain in the Services after sentence and will serve their detention in A Company, and those who are to be discharged after their sentence and will serve their detention in D Company. Different categories of detainee are kept separate throughout their detention, and will undergo different training. A Company focuses on intensive re-training similar to basic training, and can also deliver trade training. D Company focuses on pre-release resettlement training, developing skills to aid the transition to civilian life.

Whilst under sentence, the detainee will be treated as the lowest rank in his service, that is, private, able seaman, or airman, regaining the original rank upon completion of sentence unless the sentencing court also ordered a reduction in rank.

Detainees can earn remission of a portion of their sentence. All offenders sentenced to over 36 days detention will receive an automatic one-third remission. Remission for sentences of between 25 and 35 days detention is calculated using a sliding scale to ensure the detainee actually serves 24 days detention. Sentences of 24 days detention or less are not eligible for remission. The Commandant of the MCTC has the discretion to award additional remission on sentences of over 90 days detention, up to a maximum remission of one-sixth of the portion in excess of 90 days.

Once a detainee has completed their sentence and been released, they are not required to spend any time on licence or under any kind of probation or supervision. Nor are they subject to recall.

The court martial has the power to suspend any sentence of service detention for between 3 and 24 months (s. 190(2) as amended by AFA16 s6). The sentencing court will consider the following factors when deciding whether it can suspend sentence.

i. the offender can retrieve his good name without actually undergoing a committed sentence. This is often the case where there has been significant delay between the offence and trial during which period the offender has performed his duties very well and effectively rehabilitated himself;

ii. the offender has shown genuine remorse and voluntarily made reparation for any damage caused by the offending;

iii. the offender is young and inexperienced and it is clear that the offence is an isolated occurrence;

iv. the offence does not involve serious violence, or violence towards a superior officer;

v. the offender is required for important operational duties.

Any time served on remand will count towards sentence in the usual way for both imprisonment and service detention. This is calculated administratively at the MCTC or the civilian, wherever the offender serves their sentence.

Dismissal/Dismissal with Disgrace

There are two types of dismissal sentence: dismissal, and dismissal with disgrace. The primary consideration for the court is whether the offence is serious enough that the offender should be dismissed as a sentence (s.265). Dismissal is not the simple termination of an offender's employment, although that is one effect. These penalties may have severe financial consequences too.

Dismissal can be awarded with or without either imprisonment or detention, and in combination with any other punishment. If a Warrant Officer or non-commissioned officer is dismissed he must also be reduced to the ranks, the rationale being that if his misconduct was so severe as to merit dismissal he must necessarily be unfit to hold any position of authority. If the offender is a commissioned officer, their commission will be forfeit.

Dismissal with disgrace is an exceptional punishment used to express the level of displeasure in an offender's conduct in circumstances where mere dismissal cannot do so. The court should always consider dismissal with disgrace where an offender is sentenced for a serious offence committed on operations where the offence is likely to tarnish the reputation of other members of the British Armed Forces involved in that operation. When considering whether dismissal with disgrace is appropriate the court takes into account:

i. The nature of the offence;

ii. Its surrounding circumstances;

iii. The rank of the offender and the degree of responsibility that should therefore be expected of him; and

iv. Whether the sentence is necessary in the interests of the Service.

The financial impact of dismissal must be considered very carefully, and the court should be provided with full details of the offender's means including their pension entitlements. Offenders coming towards the end of lengthy service may be particularly affected. The offender will have no right to attend any resettlement courses or receive any resettlement grant. Pension entitlement will also be affected, although this varies depending on which pension scheme the offender falls under.

Dismissal/dismissal with disgrace becomes spent after 12 months for adult offenders, or 6 months for offenders aged under 18.

Forfeiture of seniority

A commissioned officer may be punished by forfeiture of seniority. This means that some or all of their seniority in their current rank will be forfeit, with consequential reduction in income and pension entitlement. It may also delay the officer's career progression as a certain amount of time in rank is a prerequisite for promotion to the next rank. The sentencing court should be made fully aware of the impact of forfeiture of seniority on an offender, bearing in mind all of these factors.

Reduction in rank or disrating

This punishment is only applicable to non-commissioned ranks, and is imposed where the offender, in committing the offences, has shown themselves unfit to hold their current rank or indeed any position of authority. Where a WO or SNCO has offended seriously enough to be sentenced to service detention, the court will also give serious consideration to a reduction in rank.

Like forfeiture of seniority for the commissioned ranks, it will have the consequence of reduced income and potentially a reduction in pension entitlement. For these reasons, it will rarely be appropriate for the sentencing court to impose a financial penalty in conjunction with a reduction in rank.

The reduction in rank will be visible and will therefore carry a certain stigma. The SP will wear a different badge of rank, and may be addressed or accommodated differently. The impact of reduction in rank as a sentence should not be understated; it permanently alters a SPs status as well as their income.

Fine

The considerations for imposing a fine are much the same as in the civilian courts. For criminal offences, the court may award a fine up to the maximum prescribed by statute for the offence. For service offences there is no maximum, except where the offender elected trial. In those circumstances the court can impose a maximum fine of an amount equivalent to 28 days' pay (s.136). A fine is always expressed as an amount of money, rather than numbers of days' pay.

The court should be made aware of the offender's means in order to ensure that they will still have enough money for their living expenses. A fine will normally be recovered through the offender's pay account if still serving, or through a Financial Penalty Enforcement Order if dismissed or discharged (s.322). In either case, the court should specify the time by which the fine should be paid. The court may order the fine to be paid by instalments, and should specify the date that each instalment is to be paid (s.251).

The court should give very careful consideration to imposing a fine in conjunction with dismissal, detention or reduction in rank, as these penalties carry significant financial consequences and reduce the offender's means.

The court can order an additional term of detention or imprisonment to be served in default if the fine is not paid. This can run consecutively to any other sentence of detention or imprisonment passed.

Service Community Order (SCO)

An offender can only be sentenced to a SCO in conjunction with dismissal, due to the service policy that community orders are inconsistent with continued service.

To be eligible for a SCO, the offender must be aged over 18 and resident in the United Kingdom. This is because the community requirements will be supervised by local Probation services following dismissal, and it is therefore important that any SCO should be phrased in the same terms as a civilian Community Order. Any breaches will be dealt with by the civilian courts.

Similar to the civilian courts, the court martial has a range of community requirements available to attach to SCOs. A Pre-Sentence Report should be prepared commenting on the usefulness of any proposed order. The court must be satisfied that the arrangements are in place for supervision of the SCO to take place.

Reprimands

An officer, WO or NCO may be awarded a Reprimand or Severe Reprimand. These penalties are simply a mark of disapproval and although they do not carry any direct financial consequences they are often imposed in conjunction with a fine.

Service Supervision and Punishment Order (SSPO)

The SSPO, made under s. 173, is an alternative to service detention available for offenders of able rate, marine, private, or airman rank. It places restrictions on an offender whilst ensuring he is available to his unit for normal duties. For this reason, it is for the CO to supervise the SSPO.

The sentencing court must specify the length of the order, which can be 30, 60, or 90 days, divided into an 'initial period' and a 'secondary period'. Each length of SSPO has a specified initial period of 14, 18, and 21 days respectively. During the initial period, the offender is not allowed to take leave without the permission of his CO, and he may be subject to additional requirements such as completing extra work up to a maximum of 5 ½ hours per day. In the secondary period, this reduces to a maximum of 1 hour per day. During the secondary period, the offender may be made subject to requirements such as not to leave a relevant place and/or not to enter a specified place without the permission of the CO. The SSPO also has a financial impact. The offender must forfeit one-sixth of his pay for the duration of the order.

Admonition

This is used for very minor offences or where there is very strong mitigation. It is loosely equivalent to an absolute discharge in the civilian courts. It may be made in conjunction with a Service Compensation Order.

Stoppage of Leave

This is a minor punishment which may be awarded by the court martial to an offender who has elected trial. It is only applicable to Warrant Officer rank and below. The maximum stoppage of leave that can be awarded is 14 days. The offender does not lose their entitlement to that eave, but may not take leave until the end of the stoppage period. The exception to this is where the start of the stoppage period is delayed for up to 28 days for compassionate or operational reasons.

Restriction of Privileges (ROPs)

This is a minor punishment which may be awarded by the court martial to an offender who has elected trial. The court can award up to a maximum of 14 days ROPs and only if the offender is an able rate, marine, private soldier, Senior Aircraftsman or officer cadet. This often involves being required to complete extra work or muster at a specific place up to 6 times throughout the day, up to a total of 5 ½ hours extra per day. The extra work must take place between 2 hours before the start of the working day and 6 hours from the end of the working day. Although the court may award ROPs, it will be for the offender's Commanding Officer to decide how they will be carried out.

Service Compensation Order (SCO)

The court may order an offender to pay compensation to a victim for any personal injury, loss or damage suffered as a result of the offending behaviour. The court must consider making a SCO in any case where it has the power to do so. The SCO can be of any amount deemed appropriate, subject to representations from both the prosecutor and the offender. Preference should always be given to a SCO rather than a fine if the offender has insufficient means to pay both. The SCO may be recovered through a s.322 FPEO, described above. The court may order the offender to serve a period of custody in default if the SCO is not paid (Powers of Criminal Court (Sentencing) Act 2000 s139(4)).

Sentencing Civilians subject to Service Discipline

Ordinarily only the JA will conduct the sentencing exercise in respect of civilians subject to service discipline. Available sentences are:

1. Imprisonment
2. Fine (payable to the relevant unit)
3. Service Community Order
4. Overseas Community Order
5. Service Compensation Order
6. Conditional Discharge
7. Absolute Discharge

CHAPTER EIGHT MITIGATION IN THE SCJS

General principles

Mitigating on behalf of an offender in the SCJS seeks to achieve the same end as mitigating for a defendant in the civilian justice system: to explain the offender's personal circumstances, the circumstances of the offending, reduce the category range as much as possible and achieve the best possible result for the client in all the circumstances. The unique environment of the military creates a number of avenues to explore that are not a feature of civilian life. As well as the usual character references, course reports and annual reports are commonly presented in mitigation. The DAO will be of great assistance in obtaining these documents.

The Board and the JA will of course be familiar with such documents, but they can initially be puzzling to practitioners unfamiliar with military terminology. The myriad potential abbreviations are too numerous to list here, but the DAO should be able to explain anything impenetrable. The next section of this chapter seeks to briefly explain the various items that you may find useful in mitigation.

Annual reports are called Servicepersons' Joint Appraisal Report (SJAR) or Officers' Joint Appraisal Report (OJAR) depending on if the subject is a member of the non-commissioned or commissioned ranks. The reports are presenting in a standard form, consistent across all the Services. The subject will be given an overall performance grade, as follows:

A+	Exceptional
A	Above average
B+	High average
B	Average
B-	Low average
C	Below average
D	Well below average

Although the B grade is described as 'average', in effect this is the grade awarded to a serviceperson who performs as expected, and most service personnel would expect to receive this grade. A and A+ grades are exceedingly rare and are therefore valuable mitigation. The reports also contain grades for specific qualities such as physical fitness, leadership, and values and standards, and will give recommendations for what the subject's next posting, course, or promotion should be.

The SJAR/OJAR contains written contributions from two SPs of superior rank to the subject. The first reporting officer (1RO) is normally the immediate superior in the chain of command, with the second reporting officer (2RO) being the next level up. The 1RO will normally know the subject extremely well, have frequent contact with them and observe their work regularly. The written section of the report will comment on particular strengths and weaknesses supported by examples of where the subject has performed a particular task or done well at something.

The SJAR/OJAR may also contain an 'insert' if the SP has recently been attached to another unit or has deployed on operational tour.

These can be very enlightening as they provide a snapshot of how an individual has performed under pressure and in an unfamiliar environment with, potentially, a different group of colleagues.

Service personnel who have deployed on operations, performed an act of gallantry, or who have been in service for a number of years are very likely to have decorations. Some SPs may have been awarded Certificates of Commendation, which do not come with a medal but are an accolade nonetheless. Where this is the case, try to obtain the citation setting out the reasons for the award so that this can be put before the court.

Service personnel regularly attend training courses, whether Phase 1 'basic' training, special-to-arm training where the SP learns their particular trade, subsequent expert trade qualifications, adventurous training, selection courses, promotion cadres, or command, leadership and management courses. Such courses are expensive to run in terms of both time and money, and they may involve great risks such as the use of live ammunition or heavy equipment. Occasionally, candidates suffer fatal injuries on training courses. Courses therefore represent a great investment by the Services into their troops, and often a huge effort on the part of the individual.

Every attendance on a course generates a course report, which may give a pass/fail or a letter grade, and will rank the SP against the cohort as well as giving written comments. The ranking in particular can be useful mitigation, for example, if the top 10% of all Lance Corporals in a battalion are streamed onto a specific course, and your client is placed within the top 10% of the course cohort, that suggests they are an exceptional member of their Service at their level.

If a SP has completed courses and done well at their training, their parent Service and chain of command is more likely to want to keep them in service, which may be reflected in any character references. This may also influence the way the Board approaches sentence, encouraging the imposition of sanctions that would permit continued service, rather than sanctions such as imprisonment or dismissal.

Operational effectiveness and employability can be taken into account as a relevant consideration when dismissal is an option for the court. This may involve hearing evidence from the offender's superior officers or CO, in addition to reading reports, references and citations.

Mitigating for service personnel in the civilian courts

Service personnel may find themselves before the civilian courts, which of course have jurisdiction over many offences committed in many situations, even with a military defendant. If the chain of command becomes aware of a court hearing in the Magistrates' or Crown Court, either because the SP has self-reported or because police have contacted the chain of command following arrest, then a DAO is likely to be assigned and will attend the court hearings. They will again act as a point of liaison for the unit and will assist counsel in obtaining any necessary documentation. Remember to obtain OJARs/SJARs/course reports as described above, as these can be useful for mitigation in the civilian courts too.

Certain sentences may have a serious impact upon the defendant's military career, which the civilian court may not be aware of. For example, if a defendant receives a sentence of imprisonment then they will also face administrative action and will be discharged from the military. This is important mitigation to put before the court.

There is a Service policy that Service Community Orders are incompatible with continued service and should not be used, and should therefore only be imposed in combination with dismissal. The same policy is likely to apply to suspended sentences and community orders imposed by the civilian courts. Even where a defendant receives a suspended sentence or community order, they are likely to face administrative action and discharge if it is found that the community requirements of any such order cannot be completed whilst performing military duties.

CHAPTER NINE
APPEALS

The Right to Appeal

There are several different types of appeal in Service proceedings. Summary matters can be reviewed by the Summary Appeal Court; this is an unfettered right of appeal allowing for the case to be heard *de novo*. A civilian can appeal from the Service Civilian Court to the Court Martial. Anyone convicted or sentenced by the Court Martial can appeal to the Court Martial Appeal Court (CMAC) subject to leave being granted by that court. The CMAC also has the power to deal with sentences referred by the Attorney-General as being unduly lenient, and cases referred by the JAG as involving a point of law of exceptional importance. Appellants to the SAC and CMAC have the right to legally aided legal representation.

The Slip Rule

Sentences can be brought back before the Court Martial under the slip rule and varied at any point in the first 56 days after sentence. This may be at the application of the parties or of the judge's own motion. Ideally, the court should be constituted as per the original hearing including the same judge and the same lay members, whether attending in person or by video link. As in the civilian CJS, the purpose of bringing cases back under this rule is to correct legal errors in sentencing.

If a convicted defendant wishes to seek a variation, an application should be made to the JAG in writing, giving full reasons for the application. The decision as to whether to list the case for variation proceedings will lie with the judge who sat in the sentencing proceedings. A refusal to list for variation at this stage cannot be appealed, but the sentence itself can still be appealed at the CMAC.

The Summary Appeal Court

The SAC comprises a Judge Advocate and two lay members, one of whom must be a commissioned officer, who together act as a tribunal of fact as well as considering sentence. The SAC can confirm or quash a finding of fact, substitute a different finding of fact, or quash or reduce a sentence but not increase it. It only has the same sentencing powers as would have been available in the original summary proceedings. Unsuccessful appellants cannot be made subject to costs orders. Decisions of the SAC may be appealed by way of case stated in the normal way.

The Court Martial Appeal Court

The CMAC is effectively the Court of Appeal (Criminal Division) dedicated to hearing appeals from the Court Martial. Although the appellant requires leave to appeal to the CMAC for an appeal against conviction or sentence, they still have the right to apply to the full court for leave if refused by the single judge. The CMAC normally sits with at least three judges, although occasionally a court of two judges may deal with appeals against sentence where the sentence is less than ten years' imprisonment.

Any party to proceedings may appeal against a ruling of a Judge Advocate in any preliminary proceedings. Any application to make such an appeal must be made in writing to the CMAC within seven days.

Any application for leave to appeal against conviction or sentence must be made within twenty-eight days of the date of the conviction or sentence. The appellant's representatives may apply for an extension of time if necessary. Grounds of appeal and accompanying authorities should be drafted and served in the usual manner.

An appeal to the CMAC may be abandoned by the appellant before any hearing of the appeal, without seeking permission from the CMAC. A written notice of abandonment, signed by the appellant or the legal representatives, should be served on the Registrar and any other party to proceedings. However, if the hearing has commenced the appeal may only be abandoned with the CMAC's permission.

The CMAC must allow an appeal against conviction if it finds the conviction to be unsafe. In those circumstances, the conviction must be quashed. In all other cases, they must dismiss the appeal. The CMAC may quash a conviction on one charge but uphold others, and substitute an appropriate sentence providing that sentence is within their powers and not more severe than the punishment originally passed by the Court Martial. The CMAC may also quash a conviction but substitute a conviction for a lawfully possible alternative charge, where they are satisfied of the facts proving the appellant guilty of that charge, and substitute a sentence accordingly. Where a conviction has been quashed, the CMAC has the power to order a retrial if it is in the interests of justice to do so.

When considering appeals against sentence, the court may quash the original sentence and substitute an appropriate sentence provided it is a sentence the Court Martial had the power to pass and that it is not more severe than the sentence originally passed. The substituted sentence takes effect from the date of the original sentence unless specified otherwise.

It is not possible to judicially review the Court Martial. However, the CMAC does have the power to direct the Criminal Cases Review Commission to investigate a matter and report back.

Decisions of the CMAC can be appealed to the Supreme Court where a point of general public importance has been identified for appeal.

CHAPTER TEN
HRA

The existence of a distinct system of military justice not subject to domestic oversight does not mean that service personnel can be treated unfairly without redress. The execution of teenage soldiers for desertion is now a harrowing memory of over a century ago, and the modern court martial system has improved considerably since the mid-20th century.

Recent developments in legislation, notably the incorporation of the European Convention on Human Rights (ECHR) into domestic law via the Human Rights Act 1998 (HRA), and the Armed Forces Act 2006, has led to greater independence within the SCJS, as well as ensuring a more uniform approach to service justice across all three services. Recent case law confirms that the system of courts-martial is compliant with the HRA, several challenges based on human rights violations having failed. However, the SCJS is still open to criticism on a number of as-yet untested human rights grounds.

In comparing the SCJS to the civilian justice system, it is easy to identify possible aspects that may be open to challenge on human rights grounds. An important aspect to remember is that a trial in the court-martial is equivalent to a trial in the Crown Court, with a Board in place of a jury. The summary justice dispensed in the Magistrates' Court, with a right of appeal to the Crown Court and the higher courts, is akin to the CO's summary hearings. The rules and procedures in place in the civilian courts are there for a reason. They are tried and tested and have developed through many centuries of law and precedent. They are there to ensure procedural consistency and safeguard fairness. Practitioners should therefore be aware that there are elements of the SCJS where defendants do not enjoy the same safeguards as their counterparts in the civilian justice system.

The Board

The members of the Board are quite deliberately selected from the Services because they have first-hand knowledge and understanding of the requirements and privations of military life such that a civilian could not. This brings an extra dimension to their decision making, and potentially makes it fairer for the defendant because the Board are better placed to understand, perhaps, why they acted in the way they did. The Board members are selected from outwith the defendant's direct chain of command, and should not have personal knowledge of the defendant. However, concerns have still been raised about the independence and impartiality of lay members.

The case of Morris v UK (2002) 34 EHRR 1253 raised a number of issues which were duly rejected, but the ECtHR did accept that there were significant concerns about the independence and impartiality of the lay members. It is important to note that this did not affect the independence of the court martial to a fatal degree but the ECtHR did comment upon the lack of legal training and the risk of outside influence. This led to the adoption of the direction now known as the Morris direction, which reminds the board of their duties, the fact that they are not reported on for their performance during the trial and that they must report any external attempts to influence them to the Judge Advocate. This direction is now given at the beginning of each trial.

Training and Role of the Board

In the Crown Court, the jury is the tribunal of fact only, and the judge will be solely responsible for the sentencing exercise; no lay person will have any say in sentence although the court may consider representations from probation, for example. In the SCJS, however, the lay members of the Board are responsible both for determining guilt and assisting the JA in the sentencing exercise. Yet they are not professional judges or legal professionals. The Board, of either three or five lay members, may not have any legal training or qualifications beyond the annual refresher training incorporating values and standards and the law of armed conflict. They may, perhaps, have experience of dealing with administrative action or summary hearings, or have previously acted as a DAO.

Following the case of Lance Sergeant Findlay in the 1990s, there was significant restructuring of the court-martial procedure leading to much better training for the Board. The case of Morris in 2002 also commented upon the lack of training of lay members. The MOD maintained that all service personnel in the relevant ranks received a certain amount of legal training. This view had been reinforced in the case of R v Boyd, Hastie and Spear, Saunby and Others [2002] UKHL 31 in which Lord Rodger of Earlsferry concluded that since there were other safeguards in place, the absence of legal training did not affect independence and impartiality. In fact, Lord Rodger went further and observed that the lay members needed no training to exercise their function as a jury. It is, of course, right to say that no training at all would be necessary if the lay members confined themselves to the role of a jury. However, they do not.

Cooper v UK [2003] ECHR 48843/99 also considered the issue of training of lay members. The Grand Chamber concluded that the independence of the lay members was not undermined by their lack of legal training but again it made no distinction between the fact-finding aspect of their contribution and the sentencing exercise. The MOD somewhat overstates the amount of training devoted to legal issues in an officer's career and it is arguable that the training is not adequate to equip a service person to contribute to a sentencing exercise.

This would not be a problem if the professional judge had the casting vote. However, by virtue of there being at least three Board members to a single JA, the views of the Board can outweigh the sentencing views of a professional judge. It is true there are parallels in the civilian justice system. Magistrates do outnumber the professional Judge when they sit as justices for appeals to the Crown Court, and indeed lay magistrates can properly form a tribunal in their own right in the Magistrates' Court. They act as judges of fact and contribute to the sentencing exercise, creating the same risk as lay members of the panel during a court-martial. However, while the problems with civilian magistrates cannot be denied, they do receive far more training and practice than service personnel.

It is acknowledged that this issue may not fall squarely within Article 6; the argument is not that there is a lack of independence as a result of the function of the lay members but that there is a risk of injustice in a system where lay members can outweigh the wishes of a professional Judge. Even with the safety net of sentencing guidelines and the possibility of appeal to the CMAC, this situation does not altogether have the appearance of fairness, lacking as it is in parity with the civilian courts.

Size of the Board and majority verdicts

Another issue for consideration is the number of lay members. In the civilian Crown Courts, the expected size of a jury is twelve jurors, with an absolute minimum number nine. In the courts-martial, the Board will be of either three or five lay members. There is an argument that a defendant is more likely to be convicted in the courts-martial compared to the civilian Crown Courts. The burden and standard of proof remains the same, but there is a smaller tribunal of fact.

Imagine trying to get a group to agree on what takeaway to order or what to watch on TV. It can be hard enough to reach a consensus with only three people, and it gets exponentially more difficult with five people, nine people, or twelve people. Similarly, it may be much easier for three lay members to agree on a defendant's guilt, whereas five, nine or twelve may have much more difficulty. This is one of the matters that defendants in either-way offences should consider when deciding whether to accept a summary trial or to elect Crown Court trial. Defendants in the SCJS have no such choice. They are stuck with the size of Board allocated to them by the court-martial.

This issue is of particular importance when a trial results in a majority verdict. In the civilian Crown Courts, at least nine members of a ten-person jury, or ten members of an eleven or twelve-person jury must agree in order to convict a defendant by a majority, requiring a majority of between 83-91%. In the court-martial, the majority can be as low as 66%.

It is understandable that the military does not want people with an attitude of entitlement but it must want to, and be expected to, treat its personnel fairly. It cannot be right that a serviceperson who risks his life to protect civilians should be in a position of disadvantage before the law simply by virtue of the fact that he appears before the courts martial rather than the civilian courts.

'A Practical Guide to the Pre-Action RTA Claims Protocol for Personal Injury Lawyers' by Antonia Ford
'A Practical Guide to Neighbour Disputes and the Law' by Alexander Walsh
'A Practical Guide to Forfeiture of Leases' by Mark Shelton
'A Practical Guide to Coercive Control for Legal Practitioners and Victims' by Rachel Horman
'A Practical Guide to Rights Over Airspace and Subsoil' by Daniel Gatty
'Tackling Disclosure in the Criminal Courts – A Practitioner's Guide' by Narita Bahra QC & Don Ramble
'A Practical Guide to the Law of Driverless Cars – Second Edition' by Alex Glassbrook, Emma Northey & Scarlett Milligan
'A Practical Guide to TOLATA Claims' by Greg Williams
'Artificial Intelligence – The Practical Legal Issues' by John Buyers
'A Practical Guide to the Law of Prescription in Scotland' by Andrew Foyle
'A Practical Guide to the Construction and Rectification of Wills and Trust Instruments' by Edward Hewitt
'A Practical Guide to the Law of Bullying and Harassment in the Workplace' by Philip Hyland
'How to Be a Freelance Solicitor: A Practical Guide to the SRA-Regulated Freelance Solicitor Model' by Paul Bennett
'A Practical Guide to Prison Injury Claims' by Malcolm Johnson
'A Practical Guide to the Small Claims Track' by Dominic Bright
'A Practical Guide to Advising Clients at the Police Station' by Colin Stephen McKeown-Beaumont
'A Practical Guide to Antisocial Behaviour Injunctions' by Iain Wightwick
'Practical Mediation: A Guide for Mediators, Advocates, Advisers, Lawyers, and Students in Civil, Commercial, Business, Property, Workplace, and Employment Cases' by Jonathan Dingle with John Sephton
'The Mini-Pupillage Workbook' by David Boyle

'A Practical Guide to Crofting Law' by Brian Inkster
'A Practical Guide to Spousal Maintenance' by Liz Cowell
'A Practical Guide to the Law of Domain Names and Cybersquatting' by Andrew Clemson
'A Practical Guide to the Law of Gender Pay Gap Reporting' by Harini Iyengar
'A Practical Guide to the Rights of Grandparents in Children Proceedings' by Stuart Barlow
'NHS Whistleblowing and the Law' by Joseph England
'Employment Law and the Gig Economy' by Nigel Mackay & Annie Powell
'A Practical Guide to Noise Induced Hearing Loss (NIHL) Claims' by Andrew Mckie, Ian Skeate, Gareth McAloon
'An Introduction to Beauty Negligence Claims – A Practical Guide for the Personal Injury Practitioner' by Greg Almond
'Intercompany Agreements for Transfer Pricing Compliance' by Paul Sutton
'Zen and the Art of Mediation' by Martin Plowman
'A Practical Guide to the SRA Principles, Individual and Law Firm Codes of Conduct 2019 – What Every Law Firm Needs to Know' by Paul Bennett
'A Practical Guide to Adoption for Family Lawyers' by Graham Pegg
'A Practical Guide to Industrial Disease Claims' by Andrew Mckie & Ian Skeate
'A Practical Guide to Redundancy' by Philip Hyland
'A Practical Guide to Vicarious Liability' by Mariel Irvine
'A Practical Guide to Applications for Landlord's Consent and Variation of Leases' by Mark Shelton
'A Practical Guide to Relief from Sanctions Post-Mitchell and Denton' by Peter Causton
'A Practical Guide to Equity Release for Advisors' by Paul Sams
'A Practical Guide to Unlawful Eviction and Harassment' by Stephanie Lovegrove
'A Practical Guide to the Law Relating to Food' by Ian Thomas

‘A Practical Guide to Financial Services Claims’ by Chris Hegarty
‘The Law of Houses in Multiple Occupation: A Practical Guide to HMO Proceedings’ by Julian Hunt
‘A Practical Guide to Unlawful Eviction and Harassment’ by Stephanie Lovegrove
‘A Practical Guide to Solicitor and Client Costs’ by Robin Dunne
‘Occupiers, Highways and Defective Premises Claims: A Practical Guide Post-Jackson – 2nd Edition’ by Andrew Mckie
‘A Practical Guide to Financial Ombudsman Service Claims’ by Adam Temple & Robert Scrivenor
'A Practical Guide to Advising Schools on Employment Law' by Jonathan Holden
‘A Practical Guide to Running Housing Disrepair and Cavity Wall Claims: 2nd Edition’ by Andrew Mckie & Ian Skeate
‘A Practical Guide to Holiday Sickness Claims – 2nd Edition’ by Andrew Mckie & Ian Skeate
‘Arguments and Tactics for Personal Injury and Clinical Negligence Claims’ by Dorian Williams
‘A Practical Guide to QOCS and Fundamental Dishonesty’ by James Bentley
‘A Practical Guide to Drone Law’ by Rufus Ballaster, Andrew Firman, Eleanor Clot
‘A Practical Guide to Compliance for Personal Injury Firms Working With Claims Management Companies’ by Paul Bennett
‘A Practical Guide to the Landlord and Tenant Act 1954: Commercial Tenancies’ by Richard Hayes & David Sawtell
‘A Practical Guide to Dog Law for Owners and Others’ by Andrea Pitt
‘RTA Allegations of Fraud in a Post-Jackson Era: The Handbook – 2nd Edition’ by Andrew Mckie
‘RTA Personal Injury Claims: A Practical Guide Post-Jackson’ by Andrew Mckie
‘On Experts: CPR35 for Lawyers and Experts’ by David Boyle
‘An Introduction to Personal Injury Law’ by David Boyle

www.ingramcontent.com/pod-product-compliance
Ingram Content Group UK Ltd.
Pitfield, Milton Keynes, MK11 3LW, UK
UKHW020150290926
15471UKWH00004B/782